This Journal Belongs To:

____